Cordilleras

Jessica Morrison

Weigl

Published by Weigl Educational Publishers Limited
6325 10th Street SE
Calgary, Alberta, Canada T2H 2Z9

Website: www.weigl.com

Library and Archives Canada Cataloguing in Publication

Morrison, J. A. (Jessica A.), 1984-
        Cordillera / Jessica Morrison.
(Canadian ecozones)
Includes index.
Also available in electronic format.
ISBN 978-1-55388-634-1 (bound).--ISBN 978-1-55388-635-8 (pbk.)
        1. Natural history--Canadian Cordillera--Juvenile literature.
2. Ecology--Canadian Cordillera--Juvenile literature. 3. Occupations--
Canadian Cordillera--Juvenile literature. 4. Ecological zones--
Canadian Cordillera--Juvenile literature. 5. Canadian Cordillera--
Juvenile literature. I. Title. II. Series: Canadian ecozones

QH106.2.B7M67 2010   j577.09711   C2009-907300-5

Printed in the United States of America in North Mankato, Minnesota
1 2 3 4 5 6 7 8 9 0 14 13 12 11 10

072010
WEP230610

Project Coordinator
Heather Kissock

Designers
Warren Clark, Janine Vangool

All of the Internet URLs given
in the book were valid at the
time of publication. However,
due to the dynamic nature of
the Internet, some addresses
may have changed, or sites
may have ceased to exist since
publication. While the author
and publisher regret any
inconvenience this may cause
readers, no responsibility for
any such changes can be
accepted by either the
author or the publisher.

Photograph Credits

Weigl acknowledges Getty Images and All Canada Photos as image suppliers for this title.

Every reasonable effort has been made to trace ownership and to obtain permission to reprint
copyright material. The publishers would be pleased to have any errors or omissions brought
to their attention so that they may be corrected in subsequent printings.

We acknowledge the financial support for the Government of Canada through the Canada Book
Fund for our publishing activities.

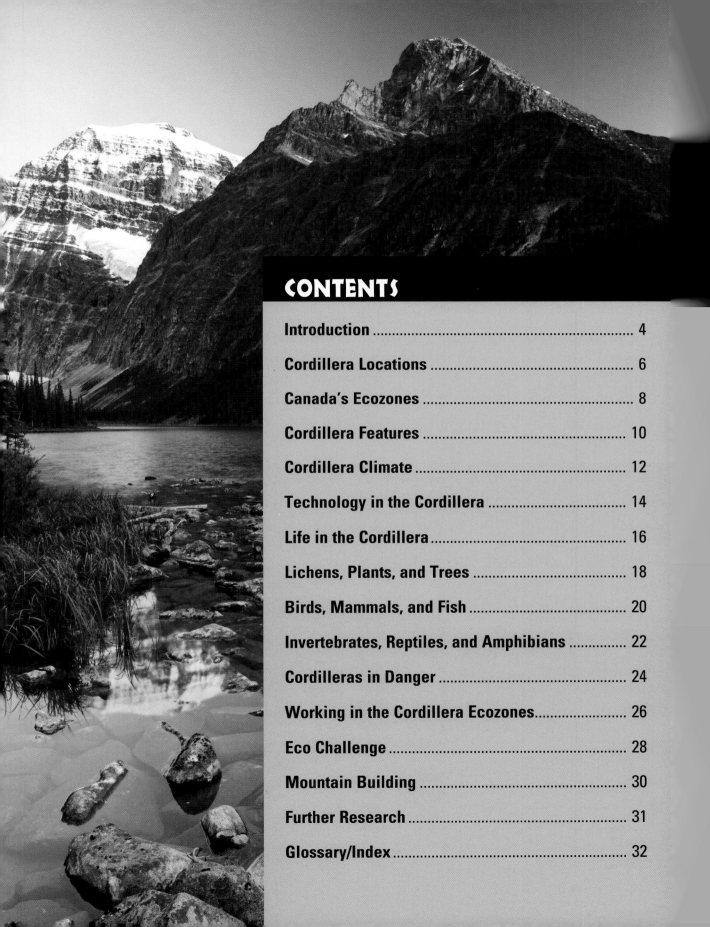

CONTENTS

Introduction

Canada is one of the largest countries in the world and also one of the most diverse. It spans nearly 10 million square kilometres, from the Pacific Ocean in the west to the Atlantic Ocean in the east. Canada's vast landscape features a wide range of geography. Yet, as diverse as the country's geography is, some areas still share common characteristics. These regions are called ecozones. Along with common geographic features, ecozones share similar climates and life forms, such as plants and animals.

Ecozones demonstrate the reliance between **organisms** and their environment. All organisms have unique survival needs. Some organisms thrive in cold, while others require hot climates. They rely on their environment to meet their needs. Just like a puzzle, every organism has its own place in an ecozone.

Crowsnest Pass, in southern Alberta, showcases the scenic landscapes of the cordillera ecozones.

Moraine Lake is located in Banff National Park. Its beautiful scenery attracts visitors from all over the world.

Canada has both terrestrial, or land-based, and marine, or water-based, ecozones. The terrestrial ecozones can be grouped into five broad categories. These categories are Arctic, shields, plains, maritimes, and cordilleras.

Covering parts of the Yukon, Alberta, and British Columbia, Canada's cordillera ecozones are some of the most stunning regions in Canada. They feature mountain ranges, valleys, and canyons, along with rivers, lakes, and some of the highest waterfalls in the country. This environment provides the survival needs of the many plants and animals that live here.

FASCINATING FACTS

The word *cordillera* is Spanish for "chain of mountains."

Canada's cordillera ecozones cover about 1.6 million square kilometres of land.

Cordillera Locations

The defining feature of a cordillera ecozone is a mountain chain. The size of the chain will be substantial, and it will often be a continent's principal mountain system. In North America, the Rocky Mountain system is the continent's major chain. As the Rockies run through the western part of the country, Canada's cordillera ecozones are found in British Columbia, Alberta, the Yukon, and the Northwest Territories. There are three separate and distinct cordillera ecozones, each having its own set of unique characteristics.

Taiga Cordillera

The Taiga Cordillera ecozone is located in the northernmost part of the Yukon and runs along the Yukon-Northwest Territories border. The northern part of the Rocky Mountain system runs

Mount Robson is located at the west entrance to British Columbia's Mount Robson National Park.

through this ecozone. Even though the Taiga Cordillera is sparsely populated, humans have lived in it for 20,000 to 40,000 years. This makes it one of the longest inhabited areas of Canada.

Montane Cordillera

The Montane Cordillera spans most of southern British Columbia and some of southwestern Alberta. It includes the Rocky Mountains, as well as the Columbia Mountain chain, which is found in the British Columbia interior. The highest mountain in the Canadian Rockies, Mount Robson, is found in the Montane Cordillera ecozone. Mount Robson stands at a height of 3,954 metres.

Mount MacDonald is one of the highest peaks in the Yukon's MacKenzie Mountain range.

Kluane National Park is the only national park found in the Boreal Cordillera.

Boreal Cordillera

The Boreal Cordillera spans more than 444,000 square kilometres across northern British Columbia and the southern Yukon. This ecozone contains the midsection of the Rocky Mountain chain, along with several other smaller chains. Most of the population of the Yukon resides within the Boreal Cordillera.

FASCINATING FACTS

The Rocky Mountains are the largest mountain range in all of North America, spanning more than 1,200 kilometres in Canada alone. The Canadian Rocky Mountains have 17 peaks with altitudes higher than 3,500 metres.

A volcano named Mount Edziza is located in the Boreal Cordillera. Mount Edziza last erupted four million years ago.

Seven of Canada's national parks are located in the Montane Cordillera.

CANADA'S ECOZONES

Canada has five major ecozone categories. Like the cordilleras, however, these categories can be broken down into specific ecozones. The inset map shows where these ecozones are located.

Look closely at the map of the cordillera ecozones. Besides mountains, what other features do these ecozones appear to have?

- Pacific Maritime
- Montane Cordillera
- Boreal Cordillera
- Taiga Cordillera
- Taiga Plains
- Boreal Plains
- Hudson Plains
- Prairie
- Taiga Shield
- Boreal Shield
- Mixedwood Plains
- Atlantic Maritime
- Southern Arctic
- Northern Arctic
- Arctic Cordillera

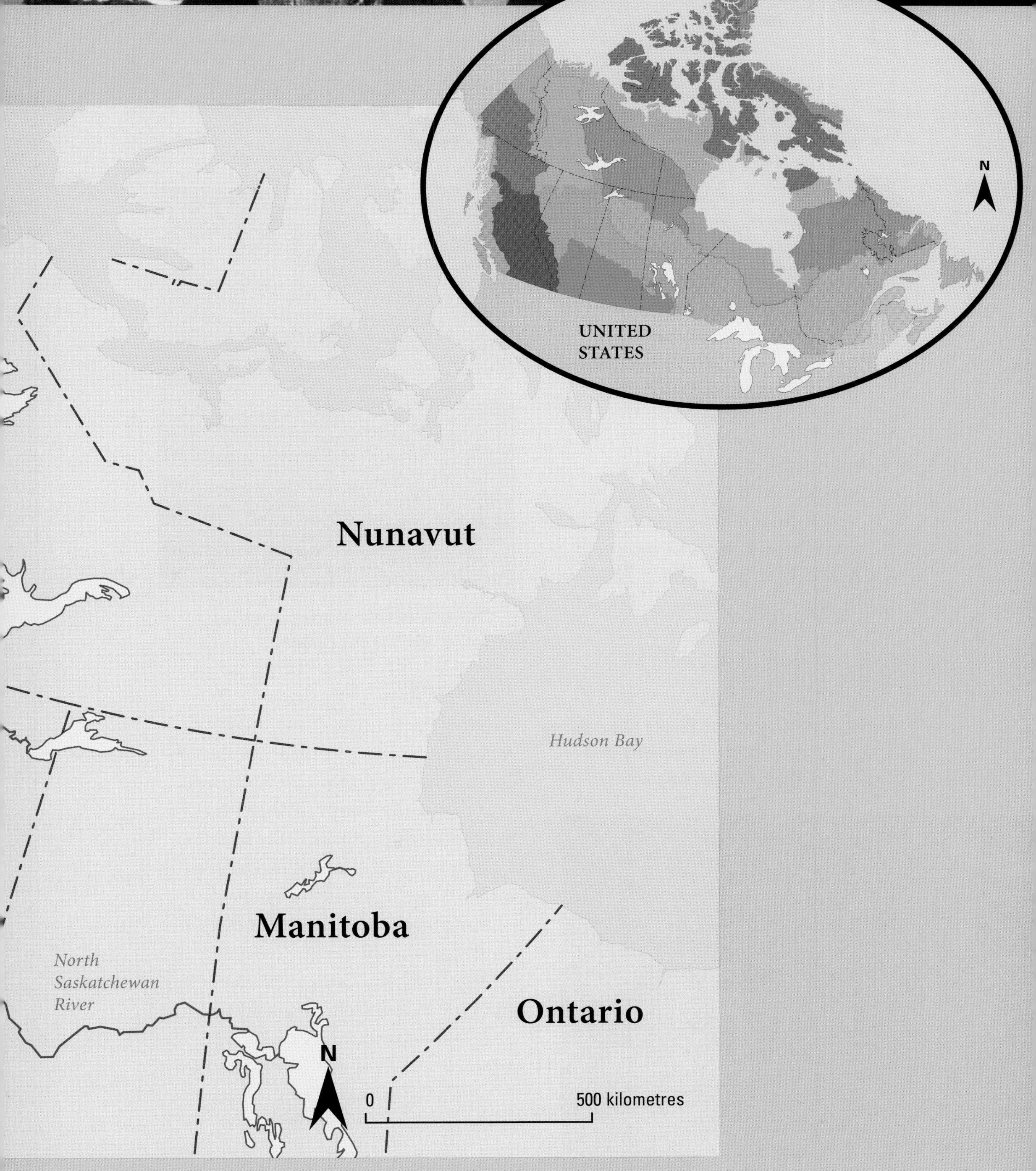

Nunavut

Hudson Bay

Manitoba

North
Saskatchewan
River

Ontario

N

0   500 kilometres

UNITED
STATES

N

Cordillera Features

Cordillera ecozones have some of Earth's most dramatic scenery. Jagged mountains that thrust high into the sky are only some of the features to decorate the land. These ecozones have a diverse **topography**, which creates a special environment for various life forms.

Mountains

The mountains in the cordillera ecozones formed slowly, between 2.5 billion to 150 million years ago. Mountains are formed when **tectonic plates** collide. These powerful collisions cause Earth's crust to bulge and buckle. This rising crust becomes a mountain chain, such as those found in the cordillera.

The jagged peaks of the Rocky Mountains stand as proof of tectonic activity that occurred millions of years ago.

British Columbia's Okanagan Valley is part of the Interior Plateau.

Plateaus

Between the cordillera's mountain ranges are a series of broad valleys and plains. These are often called plateaus. One of the best-known plateaus in the Montane Cordillera is the Interior Plateau of British Columbia. Located on the west side of the Columbia Mountains, this plateau covers the central part of the British Columbia interior. It extends about 900 kilometres from the British Columbia–United States border and covers about 376 kilometres at its widest point. This area is known for its rolling landscape and contains few mountain peaks.

The Victoria Glacier is one of the most photographed glaciers in the world.

Waterfalls

Some of the tallest waterfalls in North America are in the cordillera ecozones. Waterfalls begin as a simple stream, with water flowing over hard rock. Over time, however, the flow of the water **erodes** the softer rock underneath, causing it to break away to form a steep cliff. Water courses over the top of this cliff, landing in a **plunge pool** below. The Virginia Falls, in the Northwest Territories, along with British Columbia's Takakkaw Falls and Helmcken Falls are some of the highest and most powerful falls in the country.

The Takakkaw Falls are located in British Columbia's Yoho National Park. They are the second-highest falls found in western Canada.

Glacial Lakes and Rivers

Due to the high elevation of its mountains, the cordillera ecozones feature many **glaciers**. These glaciers are the driving force behind the area's lakes and rivers, as they store an enormous amount of fresh water. Gravity slowly pushes glacial ice down a mountain. As the ice reaches lower elevations, it begins melting and flows down to fill the area's rivers and lakes. Lake Louise, a well-known tourist attraction in Alberta, is a glacial lake. Its waters come from the Victoria Glacier.

FASCINATING FACTS

The Virginia Falls are twice the height of Ontario's Niagara Falls.

The brilliant blue-green colour of Lake Louise's waters comes from rock flour. The rock flour drains from the glaciers that feed the lake.

Cordillera Climate

The climate in the cordillera ecozones ranges widely. Mountain altitudes play a major role in this range. Tall mountain peaks can remain frozen much of the year, while the valleys and plains at the base of the mountains experience more moderate temperatures. The fact that these ecozones cover so much area is also a major factor in climate ranges. The climate found in the taiga ecozone can be very different from that in the montane area.

Boreal Climate

Temperatures become slightly warmer in the more southern Boreal Cordillera ecozone. In the northern part of the boreal region, the mean temperature in the winter remains at about −23 degrees Celsius. However, farther south, it averages to about −13 degrees Celsius. In the short summer, temperatures average 10 degrees Celsius. Precipitation throughout the ecozone ranges widely. The eastern, more mountainous, part of the ecozone can receive as much as 1,500 millimetres of precipitation in a year. Most of this precipitation falls as snow. The valleys and plains of western parts of the ecozone, including the Klondike Plateau, normally receive 300 millimetres or less. This is because of the **rain shadow** created by the mountains along the Pacific Coast.

Taiga Climate

The Taiga Cordillera is dry, receiving only about 300 millimetres of precipitation each year. Winter is difficult and cold in this area. The average temperature in winter is −22 degrees Celsius. The region's summers are short and cool, with an average temperature of 8 degrees Celsius. The cold temperatures cause snow to remain on the ground for up to eight months of the year.

In Jasper National Park, higher altitudes can receive major snowfall as early as October.

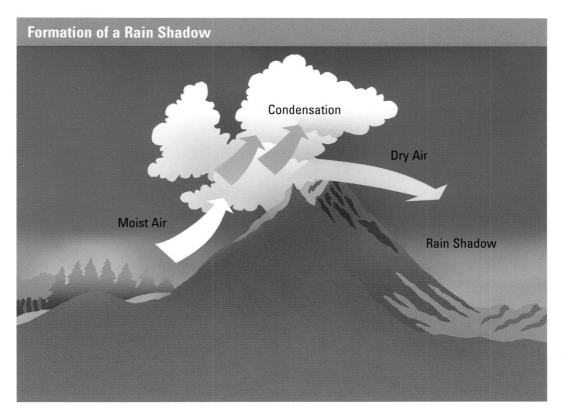

Formation of a Rain Shadow

Condensation

Dry Air

Moist Air

Rain Shadow

Mountains on the coast block air carrying water from the ocean to areas inland. As air rises over mountains, it condenses and drops rain on the slopes facing the wind. When the air comes down the other side of the mountain, it is compressed and dry. This area is called a rain shadow.

Montane Climate

The Montane Cordillera is one of the most climatically diverse ecozones in the country. This means that the weather can change very quickly, and often. In the mountainous ranges, annual precipitation varies from 1,200 to 1,500 millimetres. As in the Boreal Cordillera, the valleys and plains of the Interior Plateau feel the effects of a rain shadow. Average precipitation in this area is between 500 and 800 millimetres annually. The summers are wetter and winters are warmer in most areas, with an average annual temperature of 0.5 degrees Celsius in the north and 7.5 degrees Celsius in the southern areas. Many people live in the Montane Cordillera and enjoy outdoor activities in both summer and winter.

Technology in the Cordillera

Scientists often come to the cordillera ecozones to study the mountains. Mountains feature a wide range of habitats, land formations, plants, and animal life. By studying them, scientists learn about the history of the planet and can predict its health in the future.

Mountains are composed of rock, **sediment**, and soil. Geologists study the rock composition of a mountain in order to understand how mountains form and change. To study rock composition, geologists use both simple tools and advanced equipment. This may include a hammer, compass, and notebook, or a global positioning system (GPS). GPS is a satellite system that measures and marks different locations.

A geologist can explore mountains for minerals with the simplest of tools, such as a hammer.

Fossils in the Burgess Shale are some of the most complete fossils ever found anywhere in the world. Besides hard body parts, such as teeth and bones, soft body parts, such as muscles, have been preserved.

Mountains can provide clues about what life was like millions of years ago. Sometimes, geologists find fossils in the rock formations of a mountain. This tells them more about Earth's history and the plants and animals that lived in that location in the past. Sophisticated instruments used in these studies include ion-beam microscopes. These are used to examine minuscule particles. X-ray diffractometers are used to examine crystals. Mass spectrometers help date materials such as rock layers and fossils. Rock layers and fossils give scientists information about the land, climate, and wildlife at different periods in Earth's history.

FASCINATING FACTS

Paleontologists, scientists who study fossils, often work in the cordillera. One of the richest fossil sites in the world can be found in the Burgess Shale, in the Rocky Mountains of southeastern British Columbia. More than 150,000 fossils have been found in the Burgess Shale.

By studying the geology of the Rocky Mountains, scientists have been able to discover that, 570 million years ago, the land now called Alberta was actually the west coast of the continent. The land that is now British Columbia joined the continent only 175 million years ago.

LIFE IN THE CORDILLERA

There are many different landscapes within the cordillera ecozones. As a result, they are home to many types of plants and animals, each specially adapted to the environment in which it lives. Despite the large range in climate and physical terrain, plants and animals thrive in each cordillera ecozone.

Western rattlesnakes rarely use their rattle. They prefer to remain still when danger approaches.

REPTILES

Reptiles are not able to regulate their body temperature on their own. Instead, they depend on their surroundings, and especially sunlight, to warm them. The Taiga and Boreal Cordillera ecozones are too cold for them to do this. The Montane Cordillera, however, is home to several types of snakes and lizards, including the common garter snake, western rattlesnake, and northwestern alligator lizard.

AMPHIBIANS

The Taiga Cordillera ecozone is too cold for amphibians, but the wood frog, western toad, and Columbia spotted frog can be found in both the Boreal and Montane Cordillera ecozones. The warmer climate of the Montane Cordillera allows for a larger amphibian population, which includes several species of frog, toad, and salamander.

Western toads can be found at elevations ranging from sea level to more than 2,000 metres.

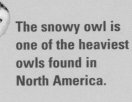

The snowy owl is one of the heaviest owls found in North America.

BIRDS

There are many bird species living in the cordillera ecozones. Songbirds, such as the purple finch, live throughout the Boreal and Montane Cordillera ecozones. Aquatic birds, such as the belted kingfisher, loon, great blue heron, and trumpeter swan, rely on the waters of the cordillera ecozones. Cordillera ecozones are also home to large birds of prey. The snowy owl can be found in the Boreal Cordillera ecozone. Bald eagles can be found in parts of all three cordillera ecozones year round.

INVERTEBRATES

There are many **invertebrates** living in the cordillera ecozones.

About 2,500 types of lichen can be found in Canada. They grow mainly on rocks, trees, and the ground.

Some invertebrates are aquatic, meaning they live in the water of streams, rivers, or lakes. Mayfly larvae live in the running and standing water of the cordillera ecozones, providing food for many other animals. The boreal cobweb spider is a terrestrial invertebrate that lives under stones and in crevasses throughout the Boreal Cordillera's forests. Although the boreal cobweb spider looks much like the poisonous western black widow spider, it is harmless to people.

PLANTS

Various species of plants can be found throughout the cordillera ecozones. All are adapted to the range of temperature and precipitation of their environment. Many plants reside at lower altitudes, but others have adapted to the cold, high-mountain altitudes. Some plants, such as shrubs, mosses, and lichens, even grow above the **tree line**, where few organisms can withstand the cold.

Lichens, Plants, and Trees

Trees and Shrubs

Altitude plays a large role in the types of trees found in the cordillera ecozones. Trees cannot grow at higher elevations due to extreme temperatures and rocky terrain. However, at lower altitudes, small shrubs, such as willow and shrub birch, can be found. At even lower elevations, white spruce, lodgepole pine, Douglas fir, Alpine fir, western hemlock, ponderosa pine, and trembling aspen trees thrive. Most of the trees in the cordillera are conifer trees. Conifer trees have needles instead of leaves, which allow them to save moisture. Conifer trees are also adapted to snow. They have flexible branches that do not break under heavy snow cover.

The Douglas fir is one of the most common trees in the Rocky Mountains.

Freckle pelt lichens are often found growing among mosses.

Lichens

Many of the areas that do not support trees are inhabited by lichen. This is because lichens can withstand cooler temperatures and need less soil. Lichens are made up of two organisms, algae and fungi, that work together to support each other. The algae use **photosynthesis** to create food, and the fungi absorb water and minerals from the ground. They share their resources, helping both to survive. This is known as a **symbiotic relationship**. Fruticose and cructose lichens are two types of lichen found in the cordillera ecozones.

Forget-me-nots bloom in late winter and early spring. They are a perennial, which means they spring from the same roots every year.

Flowering Plants

The cold climate and permafrost at the cordillera ecozones' higher elevations make it difficult for many plants to grow. However, small plants survive because they have shallow roots that do not need to penetrate deeply into the ground. Some of the flowering plants found in the cordillera ecozones include the mountain avens, Labrador tea, larkspur, and forget-me-not. Plants in the cordillera ecozones often have large flower blossoms. This is an adaptation to help the plants attract **pollinators** during the short spring season.

FASCINATING FACTS

West-facing mountain slopes of the cordillera often have more plant life growing on them than east-facing slopes. This is because clouds deposit their moisture on the western slopes before heading east. The extra moisture helps a larger number of species survive.

Trees that grow near the tree line are often **stunted**. This stunted appearance is also known as "krummholz" form. The Englemann spruce and white birch are examples of this type of tree.

Birds, Mammals, and Fish

A Canada goose can travel more than 1,000 kilometres in one day.

Birds

Birds are common in all cordillera ecozones. Some birds, such as the red-breasted nuthatch, feed on small insects within the bark of trees. These birds are able to cling upside down to trees, searching the bottoms of branches for their meals. Golden eagles are **raptors,** catching and feeding on fish, mammals, and other birds. Raptors have strong, sharp claws that can pluck prey from the sky or water, crushing it quickly and easily. White-tailed ptarmigans are small grouses that feed on willow buds. They lay light, spotted eggs that blend in well with the pebbles and rocks of their nests. These birds are also camouflaged with white feathers, helping them blend in with the snowy ground. Canada geese survive cold, cordillera waters by using a special system in their legs. Veins carrying cold blood are wrapped around other veins that carry warm blood. This ensures that the goose's body stays warm, even in cold water.

Fish

A variety of fish are found in the waters of the cordillera ecozones. Sturgeon are bottom-feeders. This means they feed off the bottom of lakes and ponds. To do this, they have developed sucker-shaped mouths to help them "vacuum" their prey off rocks and underwater logs. Brook trout and rainbow trout have sleek, streamlined bodies. This enables them to swim quickly through strong currents.

Rainbow trout are cold-water fish. They prefer to live in cool rivers, lakes, and streams.

Grey wolves are pack animals. There can be as many as 15 wolves in a pack.

Mammals

Mammals of all sizes thrive in the cordillera ecozones. Grizzly bears and black bears are **omnivores**, feeding on grubs, berries, roots, and occasionally deer and other meat. Grey wolves live in family groups known as packs. The social nature of these animals allows them to hunt prey much larger than themselves. After a successful hunt, wolves will take turns eating. They make sure pups and older wolves all receive a fair amount. Cougars are found in the Montane and Boreal Cordillera ecozones. This predator depends on the element of surprise to catch its meal. With strong claws and a flexible spine, cougars can climb trees to hide from prey. When a prey animal walks underneath, the cougar will pounce from above. Many predators, including cougars, hunt mountain goats, another cordilleran mammal. Mountain goats climb the steepest and most dangerous cliffs quite easily. They have cupped foot pads that act as suction cups along the rocks.

FASCINATING FACTS

A mountain goat's eyes have rectangular pupils. This allows the goat to see the shapes and depth of its mountain habitat. This ability can help prevent the mountain goat from slipping and falling.

The cougar has the largest legs compared to its body size of all cats. This allows it to jump long distances with little effort. Cougars can jump more than 6 metres in a single leap.

Invertebrates, Reptiles, and Amphibians

Earthworms do not have eyes. Instead, they have sensors that allow them to detect degrees of light.

Invertebrates

One of the most common invertebrates found in the cordillera ecozones is the snail. The many species found here have adapted to the various habitats. Snails live in the forests of the ecozones, as well as meadows and marshes. Snails have shells made of calcium carbonate that helps protect them from predators. To eat, they use their rasp-like **radula** to scrape lichen away from rocks. Earthworms are also found in soil throughout much of the cordillera ecozones. By ingesting soil and plant matter, earthworms help to aerate, or loosen, the dirt. This allows water to drain. In wetter parts of the cordillera ecozones, some species of earthworm can withstand being covered with water for many weeks.

Amphibians

Like reptiles, amphibians cannot regulate their temperature, so the Taiga Cordillera is too cold for them to live. More amphibians can be found in the southern cordillera ecozones, however. One of the most interesting amphibians is the wood frog. Wood frogs can form ice crystals within their own bodies as a way to survive through the winter. This process is called freeze tolerance. Basically, the frog allows its body to freeze over the winter months and then thaw when warmer weather returns. As a result, wood frogs are one of the few amphibians capable of surviving the cold climate of the Boreal Cordillera ecozone.

Wood frogs make a quacking sound similar to that of a duck.

Reptiles

Due to their inability to regulate body temperature, cordilleran reptiles are found only in the Montane Cordillera ecozone, in its southernmost tip. The rubber boa is the only **Boidae** snake in Canada. It only grows to about 73 centimetres long. This is much smaller than other, better-known Boidae, such as the python. A python can reach lengths up to 9 metres. Given its small size, the rubber boa preys on mice and small birds.

Short-horned lizards can be found in the Montane Cordillera ecozone. This reptile can puff its body up to twice its size to scare away predators.

FASCINATING FACTS

The wood frog is easily identified by the "robber mask" markings that run across its eyes and back toward its ears.

There are about 94 species of snails and slugs in British Columbia.

Cordilleras in Danger

ordillera ecozones have a very diverse natural landscape. As a result of this, they attract many people, including tourists and new residents, to the areas. When humans move into an area, they begin building structures that help them survive, play, and work. The presence of humans, and the presence of these structures, can force animals to change the way they live. Animal territories become cramped, and the animals no longer have the habitat they need to survive.

Today, urban development, ecotourism, and industry have brought humans and wildlife close together. Although it can be exciting to see animals in nature, it is also dangerous for both humans and the animals involved. Some people choose to feed wildlife in order to get a close-up view. It can seem harmless, but many animals become accustomed to humans because of this activity. After an animal becomes accustomed to being around humans, it may begin staying close to towns and farms. If it becomes a threat to the community, it may be killed to protect the humans in the area.

By removing large areas of forest, the forestry industry is destroying the habitats of many of the cordillera ecozones' plants and animals.

Industrial plants built in the cordillera ecozones often emit dangerous toxins into the air and water, making it difficult for many plants and animals to survive.

The roads and railways of provincial and national parks also remove habitat and prevent animals from moving safely from one area to another. Many animals, large and small, are hit by trains and cars.

Pollution caused by humans also threatens the cordillera ecozones and its life forms. Toxins from industry are sometimes released into nearby waters, where they are ingested by fish. These fish are then eaten by other wildlife, such as grizzly bears and wolves, resulting in high toxin levels in these animals as well.

In the Boreal Cordillera ecozone, mining efforts also impact the habitats of animals and vegetation. Mining usually occurs near streambeds, which means the water needs to be dammed or diverted. During the construction of the dam or diversion project, plants around the streambed are removed. This affects both water quality and fish habitats, even long after mining has stopped.

FASCINATING FACTS

Canada is the largest exporter of forest products in the world. British Columbia produces 45 percent of the Canadian total.

When toxins move up through the animals in a food chain, the process is known as bioaccumulation.

There were 388 mining exploration projects in British Columbia in 2008. These explorations were to search for coal and minerals.

WORKING IN THE CORDILLERA ECOZONES

Many people come to the cordillera ecozones to study the geography, geology, and life forms found in the area. Others find work in the tourist industry, showing visitors the beautiful scenery and landscapes that the ecozones offer.

GEOLOGIST

- Duties: studies rock formations and their relationship to Earth's history, makeup, and evolution

- Education: undergraduate or graduate degree in geology

- Interests: geology, paleontology, vulcanology

Geologists study the rock formations of Earth's mountains. They examine how mountains are formed, what they are composed of, and help predict future movements in Earth's crust.

HIKING GUIDE

- Duties: provides ecological information and education to families, hikers, and other groups of people

- Education: certificate or degree in outdoor recreation

- Interests: hiking, botany, zoology, ecology

Hiking guides lead tours of people through the natural areas of the cordillera ecozones. They answer questions about the landscape, plants, and animals and teach people about the ecozones. They are physically fit and enjoy working with people and exploring the outdoors.

CONSERVATION BIOLOGIST

- Duties: studies the plants and animals in an ecosystem

- Education: undergraduate or graduate degree in science

- Interests: conservation, biology, ecology, math, botany, zoology

Conservation biologists work to ensure **biodiversity** in an ecosystem. They track different plant and animal species and present their information to the government to help design laws for forest protection. Some conservation biologists teach at colleges and universities.

ECO CHALLENGE

1 What does the word *cordillera* mean?

2 What are the names of the three cordillera ecozones?

3 Where are the cordillera ecozones located?

4 What is the name of the mountain range that runs throughout the North American cordillera ecozones?

5 List three geographical features of a cordillera ecozone.

6 What factors affect cordillera climate?

7 What are three pieces of equipment used to study mountains?

8 What is an invertebrate?

9 What effect does mining have on the environment?

10 Name a raptorial bird in the Canadian cordillera.

Answers

1. The word *cordillera* is a Spanish word, meaning "chain of mountains."
2. Taiga Cordillera, Boreal Cordillera, and Montane Cordillera
3. On the western side of Canada, comprised of parts of British Columbia, Alberta, the Yukon, and Northwest Territories
4. The Rocky Mountains
5. Mountains, plateaus, glacial lakes and rivers, and waterfalls
6. Altitude and location
7. GPS, mass spectrometer, x-ray diffractometer, hammer, compass
8. An organism without a backbone
9. Mining diverts the water sources of many areas and results in species and habitat loss.
10. The golden eagle is a raptorial bird of the cordillera.

MOUNTAIN BUILDING

Earth's surface is made of a thin layer of rock called the crust. The crust is broken into 12 large pieces called tectonic plates. A river of hot magma flows under these plates. The movement of the magma causes the plates to slowly shift. Sometimes, the plates move away from each other. Other times, they hit against each other. Rocks are formed and recycled through the movement of tectonic plates. Try this exercise below to see what happens to rocks when mountains form.

MATERIALS

- foam sheets of different thicknesses and colours
- string
- scissors

1. With an adult's help, cut the foam into strips 5 to 10 centimetres wide and 20 to 30 centimetres long.

2. Cut two small holes into each end with the scissors.

3. Alternate thickness and colour to create a stack of three to five pieces. These layers of foam represent layers of rock.

4. Thread the string through the holes cut in the foam to fasten the pieces together, forming a foam sandwich.

5. Make sure the string is loose enough that the foam pieces can slide when bent. By pushing and folding the foam you can imagine how rock layers respond to the same forces.

FURTHER RESEARCH

How can I find out more about mountains and ecozones in Canada?

- Libraries have many interesting books about all of these topics and more.

- The Internet has many great websites about Canada's mountains and ecozones. Government websites are great for learning about geography in particular.

- Outdoor learning and activity centres are great places to start learning about the mountains and ecosystems of Canada.

BOOKS

Hynes, Margaret. *Science Kids Mountains*. Kingfisher Press: 2009.

Kavanagh, James. *Rocky Mountain Wildlife Nature Activity Book: Educational Games & Activities for Kids of All Ages*. Waterford Press: 2004.

Penn, Briony. *The Kids Book of Canadian Geography*. Kids Can Press: 2008.

WEBSITES

Where can I learn more about different species of animals?

Animal Diversity Web
http://animaldiversity.ummz.umich.edu/site/index.html

Where can I learn about Canada's ecozones?

Environment Canada
www.pc.gc.ca/apprendre-learn/prof/itm2-crp-trc/htm/ecozone_e.asp

Where can I learn about the geology of the Rocky Mountains?

MountainNature
www.mountainnature.com/geology

GLOSSARY

altitudes: the heights of objects above the horizon

bioaccumulation: when toxins and pollutants are taken up into the tissues of animals

biodiversity: the number and variation of life forms in one environment

Boidae: a family of snakes that constricts, or squeezes, its prey to death

erodes: wears away

glaciers: large, slow-moving bodies of ice

invertebrates: animals that do not have a backbone

omnivores: animals that feed on both plants and other animals

organisms: any living things

photosynthesis: the process by which plants convert sunlight into energy

plunge pool: the area at the bottom of a waterfall, where the water flows and falls

pollinators: organisms that transfer pollen from one plant to another, normally insects

radula: a small, scraping tongue used by snails to collect food from rocks

rain shadow: an area receiving little precipitation because of a barrier, such as a mountain range

raptors: birds of prey

sediment: the matter that settles to the bottom of a liquid

stunted: smaller than normal in size

symbiotic relationship: the relationship between two organisms that are dependent on each other

tectonic plates: segments of Earth's crust

topography: the surface features of a region

tree line: the highest point on a mountain where trees can grow and survive

INDEX